Original title:
Starlight on Frozen Water

Copyright © 2024 Creative Arts Management OÜ
All rights reserved.

Author: Aidan Marlowe
ISBN HARDBACK: 978-9916-94-488-2
ISBN PAPERBACK: 978-9916-94-489-9

A Halo of Stars on a Frozen Horizon

The lake's a mirror, oh what a sight,
Those fish up above are just too polite.
They wiggle and dance, they think they're so slick,
While I slip and slide, it's quite the old trick.

With ice cream in hand, I'll take a big leap,
But all that I land on is powdery heap.
The stars giggle bright as they watch me fall,
While I blame the moon for the whole bally call.

The snowmen nod as they witness my plight,
They've got better balance, those frosty delights.
I holler, I stumble, and laugh with disdain,
As the frozen world sparkles with frost in my brain.

So here in this realm of fun and of ice,
I'll dance with the stars, won't think twice.
With every slip, there's giggles galore,
In this crazy, cold place, who could ask for more?

Dancing Lights on Icy Swells

Beneath the moon, the ice does hop,
Like dancing penguins, it just won't stop.
The chilly breeze sings a funny tune,
As frosty sip from a laughing moon.

A disco ball hangs from snowy trees,
Where winter critters get down with ease.
In mittens and boots, they spin with cheer,
While snowflakes laugh and join in here.

Shining Veils Across the Frozen Depths

A shimmering sheet, like a silvery dress,
Worn by the pond, oh what a mess!
Frogs in tuxedos take to the stage,
As fish croon songs, and share their rage.

The chilly winds giggle through the night,
While icicles tap dance with all their might.
With each twist and turn, the laughs abound,
As ice pigeons puff their chests and sound.

Frostbitten Dreams Glimmering Softly

In pillow forts made of snowy fluff,
We dream of fun, and giggles enough.
A snowman grins, with carrots for teeth,
And tells us jokes from beneath his wreath.

The frosty air is filled with glee,
As snowflakes tickle, just wait and see!
They dance around like sprightly elves,
While giggles echo, like joyful bells.

A Canopy of Light Over a Silent Plain

A ceiling of glow, ignites the chill,
As critters skitter, giving us a thrill.
The bunnies bounce, like fluffy springs,
While the stars whisper of funny things.

With each shining glimmer, laughter stirs,
Like snowmen spinning twirling furs.
In this merry land of winter's glow,
Jokes drift along with the soft, cool snow.

The Calm Radiance of Night's Touch

In the moon's warm hug, we glide,
Penguins slip, with grace, they bide.
Snowmen laugh, with carrot nose,
While frosty breezes gently doze.

Stars giggle down from realms above,
Chasing snowflakes like playful doves.
Each twinkle whispers a silly jest,
Beneath the night, we laugh the best.

Glacial Dreams of Sparkling Night

Ice cubes skate on slippery floors,
While polar bears knock on the doors.
A seal does a jig, quite out of tune,
Beneath the watchful eye of the moon.

The frost bites back with a cheeky grin,
As snowflakes pirouette, begin to spin.
Every sparkle shines with giggly light,
Making chill nights feel so just right.

The Celestial Tides of Tranquil Light

Laughter echoes through frosty air,
As ice skaters twirl without a care.
A snowball flies, it lands with a splat,
A snowman stumbles, and oh, how he sat!

Stars in the sky are twinkling loud,
As winter's warmth gathers a crowd.
Every glitter reflects joyful cheers,
Crackling laughter shakes away fears.

Shimmers of Solitude Under the Night Sky

Cartwheeling snowflakes join in the fun,
As snowmen play tag, oh what a run!
Crystal chandeliers made of ice,
Reflect the antics, oh so precise.

The midnight snacks are frosty treats,
Polar bears sharing, no time for feasts.
Each twinkle suggests a funny tale,
As laughter dances upon icy trails.

Aurora of Calm on a Glassy Canvas

On a slick pond, the ducks slide by,
One quacks a joke, oh me, oh my!
The fish beneath just roll their eyes,
While ice skaters dance, oh what a surprise!

With chilly grins, they spin and twirl,
As snowflakes drift like a fluffy swirl.
They slip and laugh, what a funny sight,
On this glassy stage, under pale moonlight.

A Tapestry of Light on the Icy Expanse

The moon winks down with a cheeky glow,
As penguins parade with a comical show.
Their tuxedos gleam in the frosty air,
One trips and flops, but he doesn't care!

A rabbit hops by, wearing shades so cool,
As chipmunks all cheer, completing the school.
They play on the ice, with a sliding dash,
While the trees shake off snow in a giggly splash.

Radiance on the Edge of Stillness

A snowman stands with a grin so wide,
With a carrot nose and a stick for his side.
He tells funny tales of winters past,
As kids nearby giggle, oh how they laugh!

The ice reflects like a giant joke,
While owls hoot on a nearby oak.
They hoard all the puns like a treasure chest,
In this frosty land, who can resist the jest?

Stellar Ornaments on Cold Reflections

The stars wink down like little pranks,
On a frozen lake, a jester's ranks.
A dog slips over, thinks he's a pro,
While cats perched high just steal the show!

Laughing snowflakes in a whimsical flight,
As frost creates patterns, oh what a sight!
Together they dance on this shiny floor,
Under cold skies while they all want more.

Frosted Dreams in Celestial Embrace

Under twinkling skies, we glide,
Slipping and sliding with nothing to hide.
Frost bites our noses, oh what a spree,
Laughing at penguins who dance with glee.

Hot cocoa spills on my silly scarf,
I trip on a snowball, the crowd laughs hard.
A snowman grins with a carrot nose,
He beats us at snowball fights, goodness knows!

Ethereal Drip of Heavenly Drops

Icicles sparkle, a chandelier bright,
Wobbly snowmen wobble left and right.
We attempt to skate but end up in piles,
With penguins giggling, sharing their wiles.

Raindrops freeze mid-air, what a sight,
We catch them on tongues, oh what a delight!
Slapstick routines in this chilly domain,
Who knew frozen fun could feel like a game?

Shiny Solstice upon the Azure Frost

The sun's shining down with a cheeky grin,
Reflecting off ice like it's got a twin.
We twirl and we whirl, all sense out the door,
As snowflakes land squarely on mom's new floor.

Shiny and slippery, we glide like pros,
But fate has a way of exposing our woes.
Down goes the hotshot in a frosty flop,
While the crowd goes wild, no way we can stop!

Glimmering Echoes on Ice

Echoes of laughter as we chase and slide,
A playful polar bear joins in for the ride.
We try fancy moves, look cool with our flair,
Then land in a pile, all tangled in hair.

Sneaky snowflakes fall, one lands on my snout,
Tickling my nose, it's a winterslap pout.
Giggles and snorts fill the cool evening air,
As we frolic like children, without any care.

Celestial Glimmer on Icy Waves

A penguin slipped, it gave a shout,
He danced on ice, that silly clout.
The stars above just winked and laughed,
As moonbeams joined this frozen craft.

The fish below, they rolled their eyes,
Watching penguins in their tries.
With flippers flapping, they took flight,
Who knew ice could stir such delight?

Whispered Reflections Beneath the Moon

A seal, adorned with shades of gray,
Attempted a moonwalk, hip hooray!
But the ice cracked with a silly sound,
Froze in place, flippers flailing around.

The moon above was in a fit,
As critters laughed at the grand skit.
Their whispers echoed through the night,
With chuckles shared in pure delight.

Frosted Dreams of a Shimmering Night

The ice skaters wore funny hats,
Twirling round like energetic cats.
With every slip, they'd screech and yell,
Those frosty tumbles cast a spell.

A polar bear joined in the fun,
Slipped on some ice, oh what a run!
He rolled and tumbled with great flair,
Creating chaos in the cold air.

Radiant Echoes on a Chilled Surface

A snowman tried to breakdance right,
Fell on his nose, what a silly sight!
His carrot nose flew off with a bounce,
As rabbits giggled, start to pounce.

The winter nights are full of cheer,
With laughter echoing far and near.
For even ice can hold great sway,
In the dance of winter's playful play.

Reflections of Distant Worlds Below

When fish wear tiny hats and bow ties,
They dance like stars beneath the ice.
With goggles on, they do surprise,
As bubbles rise and seek a slice.

A penguin breaks into a slide,
On icy floors, he takes his chance.
He spins around, his waddle wide,
As seals join in a wiggly dance.

Crystal Waves Under a Cosmic Firmament

The snowflakes laugh, they tickle toes,
As jackets puff like marshmallow foes.
Hot cocoa spills on mittens bright,
While snowmen wear a hat too tight!

A comet's tail whips through the air,
It makes the squirrels yell with flair.
They pretend to surf on icy trails,
While the stars giggle at their fails.

Whispered Dreams of Luminous Tranquility

The moon whispers, 'Catch that snow!'
As dreams skitter on frosty ground.
A snowball fight with giggles flow,
And laughter echoes all around.

The rabbits wear their bunny suits,
In silly hats and mismatched shoes.
They hop and bounce like cute pursuits,
Creating giggles in winter's muse.

Moonlit Veils on Evaporating Frost

A polar bear in shades so cool,
Takes selfies in this chilly blight.
With penguins posing like a school,
They dance beneath the silver light.

The ice melts slowly, what a sight!
With splashes, they all start to cheer.
But watch your step! It's quite a fright,
As down goes one, with a funny peer!

Flickering Candles on a Winter Sea

The ocean winks with icy cheer,
A surfboard floats, it's quite unclear.
Penguins in tuxedos dance around,
With frosty drinks, they toast and clown.

The ships all slide, it's quite a sight,
With snowmen captains, oh what a fright!
They sail on dreams, on frosty waves,
While seagulls giggle, life misbehaves.

Light's Dance in the Winter's Mirage

In the night, glow worms do the cha-cha,
While caribou moonwalk, oh la la!
A disco ball hangs from snowy trees,
As frost-bitten squirrels bust moves with ease.

The air is filled with giggles and cheer,
As snowflakes spiral, no need for fear.
A frosty jester juggles his hats,
While owls hoot jokes to chattering bats.

Crystalline Glimmers Beneath the Twilight

A choir of icicles sings in tune,
As snowflakes dance beneath the moon.
A walrus winks, a clam does a flip,
While polar bears shuffle in a trip.

The twilight glimmers with laughter bright,
With snowball fights that go day and night.
A blender spins; it's smoothies, oh dear!
With whipped cream hats, the fun is near.

A Soft Glow Over Frigid Horizons

The horizon sparkles, a soft facade,
With beavers building igloos, oh how odd!
A snowman sneezes, his hat takes flight,
While rabbits giggle at the frosty sight.

The lights do twinkle as if to tease,
With penguins playing hopscotch with ease.
An elf slips, yells, "Ho, ho, whoa!"
While snowflakes giggle, putting on a show.

Glints of Infinity on Icy Reflections

Twinkling sparkles dance so bright,
Like disco balls in the cold night.
I slipped and fell, oh what a sight,
My flailing arms were quite the fright.

The moon laughed hard, the stars all giggled,
As on the ice my feet just wiggled.
I tried to skate, but there I wiggled,
My grand ballet? It simply jiggled.

Frozen puddles like mirrors, oh dear,
Reflecting all those snacks I hold near.
A cheeky raccoon gives a sneer,
Guess it's snack time, my friends, never fear!

With each slip, the cold air sings,
Of winter fun and all its flings.
I toss my hat; it takes to wings,
A flying snowman – oh what it brings!

Serenity's Light on a Glistening Field

In the snowy park, I took a chance,
To frolic freely, a frosty dance.
One small trip led to my big prance,
Down the hill, what a silly stance!

The snowflakes whispered little tales,
Of cocoa dreams, of hot chocolate swales.
But all I found were frosty trails,
Where laughter echoes and giggle sails.

A snowman's nose—oh what a laugh!
A carrot misplaced, like a silly gaffe.
He's giving me a funny chaff,
As if he's judging my own photograph.

So here I stand, in winter's grasp,
Creating memories, here I clasp.
With joy and fun, I'll never gasp,
For laughter's warmth inside I clasp!

Cosmic Serenade of the Winter Night

Stars above play hide and seek,
As I stomp in boots that creak.
The cold winds blow, what a cheek!
I giggle loudly, feeling weak.

Laughter echoes in the air,
As snowflakes start to tangly pair.
I trip on ice, what a weird scare,
And land with grace – without a care!

The chilly breeze teases my nose,
While creatures peek, the fun just grows.
A penguin waddles in silly clothes,
With every slide, my laughter flows.

Oh cosmic tunes, they make me spin,
The winter whimsy wraps me in.
I'll chase each star and take a win,
While slipping, sliding, grinning – grin!

Beneath the Stars, the Ice Awaits

Beneath the heavens, I arrive,
A frosty trail, I feel alive.
With every step, my boots contrive,
To turn this night into a jive.

I spotted shadows, are they foes?
No, just my friends in wiggly pose.
We claimed the ice, and how it glows,
With each failed turn, our laughter flows.

Wobbling forward, I lose my grace,
I slide and glide—oh what a race!
An icy waltz in this chilly space,
With humor's warmth, we all embrace.

So let the stars twinkle with delight,
As we steal the show from winter's bite.
No need for grace, just pure delight,
In this frozen bliss, our hearts take flight.

Night's Luminous Kiss on Crystal Seas

Twinkling lights dance on the waves,
As fish wear shades, trying to behave.
A penguin slips, what a flailing show,
Sliding down ice, saying, "Watch me go!"

The moon laughs bright, casting a spell,
As seaweed sways, no need to dwell.
Synchronized fish throw a party tonight,
Even the icebergs join in delight!

Stars pop popcorn in the chilly sky,
While seals try surfing, oh my, oh my!
The water chuckles, the night full of cheer,
Frosty festivities, we all hold dear.

With a wink, the frost takes a bow,
A balmy breeze says, "Don't sweat it now!"
On this sparkling stage, everyone plays,
As laughter echoes through the cold, bright maze.

Glacial Glow Under the Cosmic Veil

The cosmos giggles on ice below,
As snowflakes tango with stars in tow.
A walrus snorts, trying to sing,
While auroras twist, doing their thing!

With every twirl, the glaciers grin,
Playful banter where the chill begins.
Bubbles frolic, floating with glee,
In this frosted dance, all feel so free.

Frosty pixies sprite through the night,
Trading frosty tales, what a sight!
The night whispers secrets, quite absurd,
That even the cold seems slightly stirred.

Laughter echoes in the crystal air,
As everyone shares, no hint of despair.
In this shimmering realm, joy takes flight,
Beneath the alluring cosmic light.

Dances of Light on Still Waters

Mirror-like ponds catch giggling beams,
As frogs put on shows, fulfilling dreams.
The moon winks at a clumsy duck,
As ripples of laughter ride their luck.

Fireflies join in, with a glowing cue,
While crickets jive, shaking off the dew.
The water's a stage, where all have a ball,
In shimmering spheres, they frolic and sprawl.

A fish pops up, wearing a hat,
Saying, "Hey, watch this!" with a pointed spat.
Spinning in circles, they leap and glide,
On the surface of joy, these critters reside.

As the breeze whistles a tune so sweet,
Everyone sways, tapping their feet.
In giggling waves that shimmer and sway,
The night's a party, come join the play!

Ethereal Gleam Above the Frozen Depths

Above the ice, a glow so bright,
A polar bear jigs in sheer delight.
Caught in the magic, even the snow,
Starts spinning around, putting on a show.

Stars throw a rave on the frozen ground,
While ice skates whiz, making a sound.
Chubby seals plunge into the scene,
All while whales whistle their debut routine!

The frost takes selfies, capturing fun,
As auroras wave, saying, "Join the run!"
A fishing owl hoots, totally cool,
Making a splash in the frozen pool.

With mittens made of snowflakes bright,
It's a winter carnival, pure delight.
Under this gleam, laughter transcends,
Where each chilly moment just never ends.

Shining Veils of Ice and Stars

Under the moon, the ice does grin,
Glistening bright, with a cheeky spin.
Fish wear shades, in the chilly glow,
They've got style, as they wiggle to and fro.

Snowflakes dance like they own the place,
Twisting and turning with style and grace.
Penguins slide, attempting to race,
But land flat on their face, oh what a case!

Stars overhead, they wink and tease,
While icicles drip like a slushy breeze.
The cold gives us laughs, we can't resist,
Laughter echoes in the frosty mist.

So here we chill, under skies so blue,
With frozen shenanigans, all fresh and new.
A frosty party, come join the fun,
With our icy jokes, this night's just begun.

A Sea of Light in Winter's Grasp

Glittering waves in a frozen sea,
Making snowmen dance, just wait and see.
Ice skates fly like laughter in the air,
While snowballs fly without a care.

The trees dress up in sparkling gowns,
While critters prance, and tumble down.
A frosty feast, with cocoa galore,
As marshmallows float, we shout for more!

Stars poke fun, through the chilly night,
Casting a glow, a silly delight.
A seal pops up, wearing a hat,
"Why so serious?" he asks with a spat.

With frosty mugs filled to the brim,
We warm our hearts, as laughter swims.
In this sea of light, we're side by side,
Winter's jests become our joyful ride.

Secrets of the Night Beneath the Ice

Beneath the sheet where snowflakes lay,
A goofy otter holds a cabaret.
He juggles snowballs, slips all around,
Chortles echo, a whimsical sound.

The ice whispers tales from times long past,
Of penguins in tuxedos, unsurpassed.
With every glide that they dare to take,
The night giggles, it's all for fun's sake.

Stars hold secrets, they chuckle and shine,
While we slip and slide, a festive line.
The fish are cheering from below,
"Hurry up, folks, it's quite the show!"

Under the moon, we laugh with glee,
In this secret world, carefree and free.
The night wears a smile, slick as a tock,
In a wonderland filled with silly sock.

Tranquil Glimmers on an Icy Depth

The water sparkles with a grin, so bright,
Where icy penguins have taken flight.
They wiggle and giggle, frosting on lips,
As they dance and twirl with comical flips.

Chill in the air, but warmth in our hearts,
Snowflakes tumble like genuine arts.
Turtles wearing scarves, look so refined,
Laughing their shells off, lost in their mind.

Beneath the glow of a million lights,
Silly seals sing their heart's delights.
Their tunes echo loud, through ice and frost,
In this frozen world, we laugh, no matter the cost.

So raise a cup of hot cocoa, dear friend,
To laughter and fun, let's never pretend.
For in this magical night, we will stay,
With joy and giggles, come out and play!

Nighttime Jewels on a Crystal Plain

In the dark, the diamonds glint,
As penguins slip, they laugh and squint.
They waddle here, they waddle there,
With icy grace and a funny flair.

One tries to dance, but takes a fall,
Another spins, and bumps the wall.
With twinkling gems all around,
Their antics make the cold seem sound.

A snowman cracked a funny joke,
As frosty friends began to poke.
The crystals sparkled, reflecting glee,
While hearty chuckles filled the spree.

When morning comes, the sun will rise,
All sleepy heads with blinking eyes.
Yet till then, the night will play,
On this frozen stage, in joyous sway.

Glacial Veils of Twinkling Grace

Under hues of frosty blue,
The icebergs wear their sparkly hue.
With chilly pranks, they twist and twirl,
While seals applaud, giving a whirl.

A crooked iceberg took a bow,
The fish below asked, 'What now?'
With glacial flair and icy zeal,
They teeter-totter, a twisted reel.

A penguin's slide becomes a race,
As ice defines his silly space.
With frosty giggles all around,
They conjure laughter from the ground.

As stars above start to compete,
The icebergs dance, they can't be beat.
A spectacle of giggles shines,
In the night where humor twines.

A Dance of Stars on Stillness Shimmer

The twinkling dots began to play,
On glassy pools where icecats sway.
With leaps and bounds, they jump about,
While otters cheer and twist with clout.

A snowflake slips, goes for a ride,
As igloos giggle, they can't hide.
The moon looks down, it plays a prank,
Throwing shadows on the icy plank.

Feet stomping down upon the freeze,
Creating music in the breeze.
With every slip, the laughter grows,
As giggly echoes fill the toes.

When dawn arrives, they'll all retreat,
But 'til then, let the fun repeat.
In the shimmering night, we find our bliss,
With absurd joy, we can't dismiss.

Radiance Spread on Echoing Tides

Beneath the glow of moony sights,
The waves do dance with silly bites.
A seal pops up, then dives down quick,
With splashes loud, a frosty trick.

From every wave, a chuckle beams,
As icebergs float on goofy dreams.
The tides do ripple, the starfish grin,
A comical scene where joy begins.

The chilly jesters glide along,
In this bright night, they can't go wrong.
With laughter echoing in cool breeze,
They jive and twist with frosty ease.

In time, they'll bid a cold farewell,
But memories of giggles will swell.
As morning calls with a soft sigh,
They'll hold this fun beneath the sky.

Luminous Trails Across a Frigid Canvas

When winter's here and skies are bright,
The penguins glide, what a silly sight!
They slip and slide, a frosty dance,
In hilarious jumps, not a second chance.

Beneath the glow of flickering stars,
Frogs in boots auditioning for cars,
They leap with glee on ice so slick,
It's a comedy show, take your pick!

Snowflakes twirl in a dizzy spree,
While walruses juggle, how can this be?
A winter wonderland, quite absurd,
Where laughter rings, not just a word.

At times they stumble, boats without oars,
But giggles echo from distant shores.
In laughter's embrace, we all unite,
Under the cosmos, what a sight!

Frozen Whispers of the Starlit Skies

The moon makes jokes with glimmers bright,
While snowflakes giggle, oh what a sight!
Marshmallows float on icy streams,
In this winter world of frosty dreams.

A rabbit hops, then takes a slide,
While icicles laugh, can't keep inside.
They clink and chime in chilly air,
As penguins wear puffs without a care.

Mice wearing hats, all snug and warm,
Finds it funny when snowflakes swarm.
They tumble about, rolling down hills,
Chasing frozen giggles, sharing thrills.

And there on the glass, a fox in style,
Dances like nobody—oh, make us smile!
With each twinkle, pure joy is found,
In this winter wonder, laughter resounds.

Chasing Twinkles on the Glassy Frost

The squirrels prank each other in the trees,
Slipping on ice, they laugh with ease.
A chase after twinkles, dash! they run,
What a silly sport, oh so much fun!

In frozen fields where shadows play,
A snowman winks, 'Come join the fray!'
His carrot nose points to the stars,
As they giggle under soft moons and cars.

Bubblegum snowflakes, bright and bold,
As they land in pockets, joy to behold,
With each soft whisper and frosty cheer,
Laughter blooms bright, crystal clear.

In chilly laughter, all creatures meet,
To spin, to tumble, on frosty feet.
They chase the night with hearts so light,
In wintry realms, all feels just right.

Aurora's Touch on a Shimmering Sheet

The curtain of night brings out a show,
As ice skates twirl, oh what a glow!
Dancing shadows flicker and leap,
With jokes and pranks, no time for sleep.

A fox plays tag with the evening breeze,
Chasing reflections with utmost ease.
His tail a comet, bright and spry,
While fireflies laugh, oh me, oh my!

In the glow of laughter, the stars collide,
Each twinkle a giggle, a joyous ride.
Snowmen debate about hats that fall,
In this wintry theater, they entertain all.

So grab your scarves, let's frolic and play,
In this cosmic circus, hip-hip-hooray!
With every shimmer, the night ignites,
In frosty glee, we soar to new heights.

Frosted Gleams of Celestial Grace

A penguin waddled with flair,
In a snowsuit, quite the rare.
He slipped, then did a graceful spin,
Chasing his dreams with a goofy grin.

The moon chuckled from up high,
As snowflakes danced, oh my, oh my!
A snowball fight breaks the calm night,
With laughter echoing, pure delight.

Stars giggled as they twinkled bright,
While frosty critters planned their flight.
Sledding down a shimmering slide,
Every tumble, they laughed and cried.

So if you find yourself quite cold,
Join the fun and be bold.
For on the ice, hilarity flows,
With frosted gleams, anything goes!

A Dance of Light on Winter's Veil

Socks on hands, a winter's tale,
Sliding 'round, we start to flail.
With buddy's laugh echoing near,
Our clumsy moves, a joyful cheer.

The ground sparkles with a wink,
As snowmen plot and pause to think.
A carrot nose and button eyes,
Just wait till he tries to surprise!

Laughter bubbles like hot cocoa,
When a snowball flies—oh no, oh no!
With giggles ringing through the night,
We dance with glee, a frosty sight.

So let's embrace the fun we find,
With silly antics, unconfined.
Under the moon's bright, playful veil,
We'll rock this winter, without fail!

Radiant Crystals Under a Starry Skies

Sparkling gems on ground so white,
reflecting laughter, pure delight.
A snowman tries to catch some rays,
While kids create their winter plays.

Gliding past, a moose with flair,
In shades, he thinks he's quite the pair.
But slipping straight, he does a flip,
Twirling on this frosty trip.

The trees wear blankets made of frost,
While cheerful whispers echo lost.
As nighttime frolics in a spin,
Even the stars can't help but grin.

With every leap, each fun charade,
Frosty secrets, freely played.
So join the dance, let laughter rise,
As we twirl beneath the starlit skies!

Echoed Luminaries on Serene Waters

A duck with shades goes for a glide,
Splashing lightly, full of pride.
He quacks a tune, a plucky song,
As ripples giggle and sway along.

In the pond, the moonlight dances,
While froggy friends take wild chances.
They jump around in pure delight,
Joining in the festive night.

From frozen banks, a raccoon peeks,
The fish below have crafty streaks.
With giggles heard from shore to shore,
Winter mischief, who could want more?

So come along, embrace the fun,
Under the stars, we all have won.
With echoed laughs, we share this spot,
Creating memories, tying the knot!

Celestial Serenade on a Winter's Stage

In the moonlight, penguins dance,
With icy feet, they prance and glance,
They slip and slide, the show is grand,
A comedy act, all unplanned.

Snowflakes twirl like tiny stars,
As if the sky had dropped its jars,
A polar bear joins in with glee,
Singing loudly, "Look at me!"

Frosty air, their laughter rings,
Chasing after imaginary things,
Bunny rabbits join the crew,
Wearing shades, as cool ones do.

Laughter echoes through the night,
A festival of pure delight,
While frozen water starts to gleam,
They trip and fall, all part of the dream.

Shattered Stars Upon the Icebound Tides

A clumsy seal hops on the shore,
Slipping, sliding, wanting more,
Looks up and winks at nearby stars,
"I've got more moves than all of you, Mars!"

The icebergs chuckle, shake and sway,
As cheeky otters join the play,
They juggle fish in a fancy show,
Bored snowmen cheer, "Come on, let's go!"

Melting jokes on winter's stage,
Fluffy ramblings fill each page,
A squirrel with shades, oh what a sight,
Says, "I've got jokes that shine so bright!"

While comet tails tickle the ground,
All creatures dance in circles round,
Backflips on ice, what a delight,
Under a moon, what a funny sight!

Celestial Ripples on Frozen Tranquility

A frosty lake with laughter hides,
As squirrels skate with bustling strides,
One takes a fall, it makes a splash,
"Look at me!" he yells with panache.

The stars giggle as they twinkle down,
While a moose waltzes, dons a crown,
With ice cream cones made from snow,
They slurp and sigh, what a show!

Turquoise ripples swirl and spin,
As the snowflakes start their din,
Penguin pranks and playful cheers,
Would make even the grumpiest peer.

Giggling echoes through the night,
Each ripple shines with sheer delight,
An endless dance on crystal glows,
A winter tale that humor sows.

Night's Brushstrokes on a Glimmering Canvas

Midnight paints a wondrous scene,
With wobbly gnomes in their routine,
Slipping past the frosty trees,
They trip on roots, falling with ease.

A star-dusted brush in hand,
Creates a masterpiece so grand,
A yeti tries to take a peek,
"Is it art or just hide-and-seek?"

Bubbles of laughter fly around,
As blizzards twirl with a silly sound,
Chirpy birds in sweaters bright,
Sing silly songs with all their might.

The canvas laughs despite the cold,
With stories of the brave and bold,
As winter giggles through the night,
Under stars that twinkle with delight.

Crystalline Lights in a Winter's Solitude

In the twilight's chilly grip,
Penguins slip, but they don't trip.
Skating ducks with elaborate flair,
Doing pirouettes, unaware of despair.

Snowflakes chuckle, tumble and glide,
While frosty friends take a slippery ride.
Chatty snowmen share silly tales,
While ice-cream cones slip off the scales.

Tiptoe, hop, don't crack the glass,
As penguins bow for the icy mass.
A dance of joy 'neath twinkling crew,
With snowy waltz, the night feels new.

Giggles echo, a frosty cheer,
As icicles sway like puppets near.
Laughter rings in the chill of night,
In this frozen world, all feels just right.

The Quiet Symphony of Distant Stars

Beneath a blanket so crisp and bright,
Fuzzy squirrels join the starry fight.
They chirp and chatter, harness a sound,
While snowflakes flop like they've lost their ground.

A plump cat lounges, tail in the air,
As rabbits engage in an ice-fishing dare.
They catch a cold and giggle with glee,
Squeaking jokes to the bald, bemused tree.

Shooting stars bring a wish or two,
"Make me dance like a fool, will you?"
Beneath the moon, the laughter beams,
While snowballs fly to shatter sweet dreams.

Distant twinkles play a mischievous tune,
As owls yawn late under the balloon.
In this serene space, all seem quite free,
Twirling about in wild jubilee.

Radiant Traces on a Veil of Ice

Frogs in hats, spinning frosty tales,
Tip-tap dancing with icy gales.
They leap and glide, a sight so sweet,
Hopping around on chilly feet.

A ballet of snowflakes, each wears a grin,
Sprinkling joy when they swirl and spin.
One twirled so high, it tickled the sun,
Fell on a squirrel; their laughter begun!

Ice skates squeaked as they danced along,
With frosty legs in a jolly throng.
A snowman cheered, cape flying wide,
Held up a sign, "No need to slide!"

While winter's whisper hums low and clear,
Laughter echoes with every cheer.
Joyful chaos in the moon's embrace,
As whimsy traces in a magical space.

Luminescent Images on the Still Abyss

Under the moon, a dance does break,
With icy slips, and puffy flakes.
The jellybeans roll on their ice domain,
Sliding about like faces in pain.

A gopher with goggles leads the parade,
While penguins huddle, their dance upgrade.
What's this madness? Chatter and squeal,
In this frozen place, all join in a reel.

Stars above wink in mismatched glee,
As owls squawk out a light symphony.
Frosted giggles spin 'round like a hat,
Every creature joining, imagine that!

With giggles and howls through the frosty night,
They twist, they turn, in a shimmering flight.
Laughter looms large, like a bright chorus,
In this wild wonder, nothing can bore us!

Illumination in the Chill of Night

The moon did slip on icy beams,
It tripped and fell, or so it seems.
Penguins laugh beneath the glow,
Waddling round, they steal the show.

A frosty breeze blew flipping hats,
The owls hoot back, "What's up with that?"
Snowflakes dance, a little fleet,
While rabbits hop to find a treat.

A narwhal lost in laughter's song,
Swims past a seal—what's going on?
Each shimmer winks with gleeful flair,
No one can resist the chilly air.

As stars twirl high in a frigid spree,
Each glint a tickle, a playful glee.
With every crunch beneath their feet,
The night's a punchline, crisp and sweet.

Frozen Glimmers Under Cosmic Canopy

Twinkling diamonds in the frost,
Look up and see, it's worth the cost.
A penguin slips, and whoops a shout,
The show's begun, come check it out!

Beneath this vast, galactic quilt,
Skiers tumble, that's our guilt!
Synchronized falls, what a thrill,
Oops, lost my lunch, but what a spill!

The ice may crack, but never mind,
The stars have got comedic grind.
With every slip and snowy face,
Laughter echoes, fills the space.

So grab a cup and sip it slow,
Frozen glimmers steal the show.
Tonight's a jest in chilly ways,
Where laughter sparkles and plays.

The Night's Cloak Over the Glassy Expanse

Draped in night's soft, chilly drape,
Sleds go flying—what a scrape!
Children giggle with frosty breath,
While ice skates dance, as if at a fest.

A comet zooms with a cheeky swoosh,
Plowing through a frosty bush.
Nearby a bear tries to slide,
Lands with a thud—oh, what a ride!

Bubbles freeze as laughter peels,
What joy this winter madness feels.
As snowflakes tickle rosy cheeks,
The night is full of fun techniques.

With every glimmer, every grin,
We revel, spins and slips begin.
So grab a friend, don't let it stop,
For in this place, we all will hop.

Fractals of Light on Frigid Waters

Underneath the shimmering frost,
A fish comes up, confused, then lost!
The glow does dance, its scales a tease,
He grins wide, "Hey, freeze, don't sneeze!"

The frozen pond, an icy stage,
Where quacking ducks perform with rage.
"Watch us glide, we're very slick!"
They trip and flop, it's quite the trick.

Snowmen bicker over the light,
"Hey, I see more! You lost that fight!"
A star fell down to break the tie,
But bounced right back, "Oh my, oh my!"

So gather 'round for tales of cheer,
The fractals laugh, the night is here.
In every twinkle, every jest,
Is winter's charm—our very best.

Chilled Echoes of Luminous Wonder

In the night, a face does gleam,
Cracking ice with a silly dream.
Fishes giggle, swim with glee,
Who knew cold could be so free?

Snowflakes laugh, they swirl and twirl,
Dancing 'round in a frosty whirl.
Penguins slide, a comedic race,
Wishing for a warm embrace.

Stars above engage in jest,
While silly seals plan a fest.
They throw iceballs, splashing loud,
A winter circus, oh so proud!

Giggles echo on frozen ponds,
As we find joy in harmless fronds.
Laughter binds our chilly crew,
In this frosty world we skidoo!

Silver Threads Across Frigid Waters

A fishing rod, a hopeful cast,
Who knew the fish could swim so fast?
Reeling in an icy shoe,
"Oh wait, it's just my friend named Stu!"

Silver glimmers dance and play,
While polar bears join in the fray.
They slip and slide, take a tumble,
In this shiny land, they mumble.

Nights ignite with laughter's glow,
As icebergs stand in a row.
A walrus joins a conga line,
With flippers flapping, oh so fine!

Chilly breezes tickle the cheek,
Making all the tigers squeak.
With laughter echoing all around,
In this frosty playground, joy is found!

The Gentle Waltz of Light and Ice

Under the moon, the ground does shimmer,
With frosted jokes that never dimmer.
A froggy hops in frozen flair,
Singing loudly, "I don't care!"

Ice skates squeak a merry tune,
As penguins prance 'neath the silver moon.
Slipping here, a chubby fall,
They giggle, grace distorted, all!

Stars waltz slowly, dipping low,
As frigid winds dost catch a blow.
A bear in shades attempts to skate,
But ends up just a funny date!

The night is young, the ice aglow,
With frosty friends, we all bestow,
Laughter with each chilly fling,
In this frozen world, joy we bring!

Petals of Light on Frozen Petals

Bright blooms freeze in moonlit laugh,
As daffodils take a chilly bath.
"A bit too cold!" a tulip sighs,
Yet, in this freeze, they still surprise!

A butterfly in a winter coat,
Dreams of flowers, but can't emote.
With each flap, it spins and twirls,
Chasing snowflakes, a dance in swirls.

Crystals form upon each cheek,
Nature's giggle, perfect and sleek.
A frosty breeze makes petals sway,
"Who ordered ice for springtime play?"

Underneath the frosty map,
Life abounds in a frosted nap.
As petals shine in the moon's embrace,
We share the laughter in this space!

Breath of Light on a Pristine Surface

A glow from above, it makes me grin,
Reflecting off ice, where no fish have been.
I skid and I slip, a dance unforeseen,
This frozen ballet, a slapstick routine.

The moon's got jokes, I'm sure it can see,
As I flail with grace, like a falling tree.
A shimmer so bright, it tickles my nose,
And paints frosty scenes where comedy grows.

The surface is slick, a tricky affair,
I laugh as I stumble, it's all in the air.
With each blurry glide, I'm lost in delight,
Who knew that cold spaces could feel so just right?

When winter comes calling, I glide and I sway,
In a world made of laughter, we frolic and play.
I dream of a time in this shimmering dome,
Where icy adventures feel just like home.

Dreaming in the Light of Frozen Seas

An icy expanse, a dazzling sight,
I chase my own tail under the moonlight.
Sparkles in clusters like jokes on a roll,
The frosty surface, it plays tricks on the soul.

The penguins are laughing as I take a dive,
My flippers are flailing—oh, how I survive!
I slip on my belly; it's quite the affair,
Who knew frozen fun could lead to despair?

I see the auroras, they wink and they wag,
As I tumble and twirl, feeling quite like a rag.
Each twist that I take, a giggle I hear,
Winter's slapstick dance brings both joy and some fear.

Dreams on this ice are a hoot, what a ride,
With snowballs a-flinging, laughter's my guide.
In this world of chill, where humor is free,
I find endless joy on this frozen spree.

Moonlit Spells on an Icy Realm

The moon casts a spell on the glistening frost,
While I frolic and tumble, dignity lost.
With each little slip, I become quite the show,
In my winter wonderland, I'm the star of the glow.

I skate with a flair that's all out of sync,
As giggles erupt, and I start to rethink.
Ice flowers are blooming beneath my two feet,
A messy performance, but oh, it's a treat!

The cosmos above seems to burst into glee,
As ice crackles softly; it sings to me free.
A banter with snowflakes, they twirl and they tease,
And I join in the laughter, a flurry of ease.

So here in this realm where the chill meets the light,
I embrace every slip, it's unruly yet bright.
With starlit companionship, all my woes seem small,
As the universe chuckles, we dance through it all.

Celestial Patterns upon the Winter's Rest

In the chilly silence, I hear a soft cheer,
As the cosmos above winks down with some beer.
The patterns they make, like the giggles of stars,
I prance on the ice, with my friends from afar.

Frosty confetti falls from the night sky,
And I launch a snowball—oh my, oh my!
With each snowy blast, comes a bright, hearty laugh,
As I slip on my back, oh, what a gaffe!

Celestial antics, a vast frozen sphere,
While the wind carries whispers, I dance without fear.
Laughter in snowflakes, a jolly refrain,
While winter's cold hands wrap me snug in a chain.

Each sparkle a chuckle, each drift a delight,
In this kingdom of frost, I'm silly but bright.
So here's to the moments where ice meets the jest,
Celebrating the joy on winter's cold chest.

Twilight's Brush on a Glassy Surface

A penguin slides with style and grace,
Looking for fish at a rapid pace.
But oh! He lands in a snowbank soft,
With a twirl and a splash, he's airborne aloft.

Stars above giggle at his blunder,
As he flaps his wings like a clumsy thunder.
The ice cracks a joke, it's quite absurd,
Even the snowflakes can't help but stir.

With each wobble and hop, he makes a scene,
A frosty ballet, all sparkly and keen.
He'd tell them to watch, if he could but dance,
But mostly he's busy taking a chance.

When night creeps in and the cold winds blow,
The jolly little penguin steals the show.
With his mirrored stage, he dances bright,
Under the chuckling moonlight tonight.

Twinkling Secrets Beneath Frosty Veils

Under the ice, the fish have a party,
They wiggle and giggle, oh aren't they hearty?
They think they are hidden, beneath all the frost,
But a curious seal has a plan for the cost.

With a wink and a dive, he makes quite a splash,
The fish scatter wide, oh what a mad dash!
Each little fin thinks it's the end of the fun,
But the seal just grins, this is all in good run.

A glittery crab pulls a party hat tight,
With dance moves that twinkle under the night.
The seal joins the beat, they have quite a ball,
While stars above shine, they dance in the hall.

What's this? A hare has come along too,
He hops on the ice like it's made of goo.
The fish all stare, their secret now blown,
Under frozen veils, new friendships are grown.

Whispering Glows in the Winter's Heart

The moon spills silver on a blanket of white,
A raccoon peers out, what a marvelous sight!
He wears a big mask, ready for mischief,
While snowflakes swirl, they become his chief.

With a pitter-patter, he dances around,
Stealing some snowballs, oh what a sound!
His giggles escape with the soft winter breeze,
As he tosses the snow, 'Oh, won't you please?'

The frozen expanse plays tricks on his feet,
He slips, and he slides, what a comical feat!
The laughter of stars erupts in the sky,
While the raccoon just grins, and waves them goodbye.

In the glimmering light, he finds a warm spot,
Where snowmen are gathered, oh what a lot!
He joins in their talk, a furry-shaped part,
Together they share in the winter's sweet heart.

Radiance Captured in Liquid Stillness

A fish with sunglasses glides through the chill,
With style and sass, he's got quite the thrill.
He poses for selfies, with bubbles aligned,
"Look at me sparkle, I'm one of a kind!"

The ice above glistens, a canvas so fine,
Reflecting his moves, he dances in line.
He swirls and he twirls, strikes a pose for the crowd,
While penguins and seals cheer, all joyfully loud.

But oh! What's this? A fisherman's net,
The glimmering fish dons a look of regret.
With a flip of his tail, he makes a retreat,
Leaving behind puddles, oh what a feat!

The stars all chuckle, as he zooms away,
"I'll be back for encore, just not today!"
In the still of the night, the lake keeps its shine,
With tales of his antics forever entwined.

Twilight's Sparkle on a Thawing Dream

The moonlit jig on frozen lake,
A penguin slips, oh what a quake!
The stars cheer in a giggling spree,
While snowballs dance like they're carefree.

I skated by, my grace unknown,
My legs took flight, my face like stone!
A comet's tail of flailing arms,
Oh, how this ice holds such strange charms!

A polar bear dons a sparkly hat,
Complaining loudly, 'This won't fit at!'
He slips and slides with cousin's glee,
As frosty giggles climb a tree.

In twilight's glow, our joy takes flight,
With frosty friends, we dance all night!
A balmy cheer, a winter's glee,
As ice turns to foam—come laugh with me!

Frost and Radiance in Silent Harmony

Glistening flakes in a frosty swirl,
A snowman's hat, oh what a pearl!
With carrot nose, he takes a leap,
Into a snowbank, oh, what a heap!

The jackets squeak, the boots do clunk,
While squirrels fistfight with a junky trunk.
They stash their treasures on frosty leaves,
Making winter mischief, oh how they tease!

A gleaming star now guards the floor,
A seal pretends to be an old matador!
With flips and tricks, it winks and beams,
While I just giggle and sip my creams!

Oh, laughter's echo on the chilly air,
With frozen brooks that dance and stare—
The harmony of frost and fun,
Together under the warming sun!

Celestial Beads on a Winter Mirror

A twinkling laugh on a chilly night,
The ice looks bright, oh what a sight!
I juggled snowballs with glee and flair,
One hit a tree, it lost its hair!

The stars drop laughs from their velvet space,
As snowflakes pirouette, a dizzy chase.
A rabbit hops in glittery socks,
With every bounce, he giggles and talks!

A wise old owl in a top hat perched,
Said, "Mind your step, or you'll get searched!"
He winked, and sideways spun his tale,
While frozen streams began to wail!

So weave your dreams in frosty rows,
With celestial beads where laughter flows.
For in this dance where joys unfold,
Winter's secrets turn bright and bold!

Shimmers of Hope on the Icebound Blue

In icy tides where giggles glide,
A walrus slips with utmost pride!
His flippers flail, creates a scene,
While laughing eagles cheer, 'You're keen!'

Ice cubes clink in cups of cheer,
As frosty friends draw even near.
We toast to dreams that swirl and spin,
In shiny cups with frosty gin!

A playful fox in boots of red,
Declared a rule: 'No tears,' he said!
With every slip and every cheer,
We spread the warmth, have no more fear!

So let the blues twinkle and roam,
As we create a frosty home.
With every giggle, hope breaks through,
On our icebound dreams, so fresh and new!

The Tranquil Luminance of Icy Dreams

In a winter wonder, chilly and bright,
Penguins slide heartily, oh what a sight!
Snowflakes twirl down like ballerinas,
While snowmen joke, wearing their subpoenas.

Icicles dangled like frozen jokes,
Making the squirrels laugh, oh what pokes!
A cat in a scarf, with a frosty meow,
Trying to catch snowflakes, but don't know how!

The moon winks down, it's got a bright grin,
As frosty creatures hold an icy chin.
With every twirl, laughter echoes in glee,
Winter's dance party, come join in with me!

So cheer with the frost without any fear,
While we sip hot cocoa and toast to the year!
Under the giggles of a shimmering night,
Let's bounce on this ice, till morning comes bright!

Glacial Nightscapes Illuminated

Chilling and thrilling, here come the deer,
With antlers like disco balls, never fear!
They prance 'round the lake, doing the cha-cha,
While the fish poke their heads, "Hey, look at ya!"

The stars are giggling, they wink from above,
Casting icy shadows, in the night they shove.
A snowman sneezed, and what a big blast,
All frosty friends tumbled, oh what a cast!

A moose in a tutu, dancing with flair,
Ice-skates on paws, twirling through the air.
Penguins in tuxedos sip chilly delights,
Amidst glacial laughter, long into the nights!

The aurora glows in laughter-filled hues,
As we join the fun wearing silly blue shoes!
With each snowy flake, another giggle flies,
In this glacial wonder, under moonlit skies!

Serene Illumination on Winter's Pool

Beneath the crisp surface, shadows come alive,
The ice fish are discoking, learning to jive!
With each little crack, the fun starts to grow,
The river is chuckling, "Hey, don't go slow!"

A polar bear spins in a stylish ice dress,
While kittens on skates cause unending mess!
The owls are hooting in hilarious tones,
As laughter erupts from their icy cold thrones!

Snowflakes tickle noses, laughter ignites,
While frosty sprites share their giggly sights.
Glimmering moonbeams keep dancing around,
Making shadows twist, with joy they abound!

So join all the critters, with smiles so grand,
As winter's own whimsy waves a merry hand!
In this coolery realm, where craziness thrives,
Under glimmering scenes, let joy come alive!

Frozen Fantasies Under Twilight's Gaze

In a snowy glade, where the owls play chess,
A mammoth in slippers will surely impress!
With each silly slope, laughter fills the air,
While snowflakes dance down, without a care.

The bunnies all giggle, stuck in a pile,
Trying to hop, with their grimacing style!
A seal on a surfboard, what a grand show,
Waving at seals, "Look at me glow!"

While the stars make faces, sparkly and bright,
The snow is a canvas for a snowman's delight.
Glides on the ice, all wrapped up in glee,
With the moon as our DJ, come spin with me!

So here's to the laughter, the snowball fights,
To snowy adventures on chilly nights!
In this magical realm, all frozen and bright,
Let's dance and let giggles shine through the night!

Icy Reflections of a Distant Galaxy

The stars slipped on ice for a clumsy dance,
They twirled and they twinkled in a fanciful trance.
A comet yelled, "Watch out, you're too close!"
As planets slipped by like a merry ghost.

Frosty giggles filled the crisp, night air,
As meteors tumbled, unaware of their flair.
"Hey, catch me!" cried one, 'fore it landed with a flop,
While the Milky Way rolled, laughing nonstop.

The constellations argued where to put their jest,
While fluffy snowflakes joined, doing their best.
"Who's the king of space?" a star said with glee,
But all they did was bump bodies, not decree.

So up above in that cosmic ballet,
The ice beams reflected their light in a play.
With chocolate comets and a sparkly sight,
They boogied till dawn, oh what a night!

Celestial Luminosity on Winter's Breath

In the chilly air, the moon made a grin,
As frosty squirrels danced, dressed up in thin.
Stars tossed snowflakes like confetti in fun,
Making snowmen giggle, till their noses would run.

The North Star cracked jokes, got everyone them laughing,
While nearby a snowdrift hid a penguin's gaffing.
"Look at me!" they cried, slipping near a pole,
They spun 'round and 'round, it was all out of control!

When icicles chimed and painted the trees,
The auroras wiggled like they danced in the freeze.
"Is it blue or green?" a star asked in sweat,
As laughter erupted, no sign of regret.

So as night drew close, with a curtain of chill,
The giggles and warmth gave the cold a sweet thrill.
In this sparkling world, with each frosty chase,
Ice-skating stars twinkled, in a comical race!

Ethereal Glow of Frozen Echoes

In a mountain of frost, the echoes took flight,
Bouncing round snowdrifts, giggling with delight.
"Do you hear that?" whispered a snowflake so spry,
As it twirled in the cold, nearly touching the sky.

Frozen fish in lakes started to chuckle,
With each bubble pop, oh the giggles would buckle.
Echoes flung jokes, like snowballs to send,
While the clouds took a break, to share and to blend.

The light beams were ticklish, they shimmered and shone,

As the universe chuckled at winter's own throne.
"Why did the comet bring a snow shovel?" they asked,
"To clear a path for friends!" was a punchline unmasked.

So remember tonight, in the chill of the air,
To laugh with the stardust and offer a flair.
When winter gets cozy, and it glimmers so neat,
Just laugh with the cosmos, it makes life complete!

The Night's Mirror in a Frigid Realm

In a land where the ice rumbled under bright beams,
The night mirrored laughter, or so it all seems.
Frogs clad in snow gear skated in leaps,
Making all of heaven spill giggles and peeps.

A star said, "Hey, that ice is a bit thin!"
While comets just chuckled, afraid of a spin.
With a splash and a crash, they all made a view,
Creating a scene that was laugh-out-loud new!

As the chilly moon watched, sipping on tea,
The snowmen were plotting a mock jubilee.
Their noses of carrot exchanged frosty high-fives,
As they wobbled and bounced, with their gleeful lives.

This frigid realm glows with each silly yelp,
As the heavens perform with each shimmering kelp.
So gather your joy, let your laughter take flight,
Painting the cosmos with giggles at night!

Enchanted Light Over a Chilly Expanse

A penguin slipped on ice so bright,
He thought he'd learned to fly that night.
With flippers flailing, oh what a sight,
He landed softly, what a delight!

The moonbeams danced on water's skin,
A fish popped out with a cheeky grin.
"Come join me for a splash or spin!"
But all the seals just laughed within.

Snowflakes tickled noses and toes,
As polar bears wore fancy bows.
They twirled and whirled in clumsy prose,
Their laughter echoed, the fun it grows!

So let the chill bring joy to all,
In winter's waltz, we have a ball.
With every slip, and every fall,
We'll dance and laugh, answering the call!

Stardust Reflections in a Winter Dream

The owls hoot jokes from high in trees,
While rabbits hop, avoiding sneezes.
In frosted fields, they share some cheese,
While wishing for a winter breeze.

A snowman grinned with a carrot smile,
He wobbled proudly, all the while.
"I've got some style, can you decipher?"
But all he got was a laugh, oh riper!

Two foxes played a game of tag,
While snowflakes fell, they gave a brag.
"Catch me if you can!" one said with a wag,
But tripped on ice, what a total drag!

The stars above began to twinkle,
As critters danced and hearts did sprinkle.
In winter's fun, they never crinkle,
A joyful night, on dreams they mingle!

Frosted Dreams Beneath Cosmic Glow

A squirrel adorned in a red scarf bright,
Rushed forth to impress, full of delight.
But slipped on ice, oh what a fright,
He pirouetted and took flight!

With a shout of glee, he spun around,
As stars above shared laughter sound.
The critters gathered on frozen ground,
To witness where fun and frost were found.

A llama in boots, prancing with flair,
Stole the show, but found it unfair.
"Snowball fight!" he shouted with care,
Yet landed headfirst in a chilly lair.

And as the night wove its chilly thread,
With silly antics, no one felt dread.
Together we laughed, on dreams instead,
In a frosty world where joys are spread!

Glacial Harmony in Night's Silence

A walrus sang a holiday tune,
Beneath a sky adorned with moon.
His voice was off, but no one marooned,
As all the seals joined in, immune!

A moose with shades struck a dance,
With smooth moves that left no chance.
A snowball whizzed, he lost his pants,
While laughter echoed in a trance.

Ice skates glittered on frozen ponds,
As beavers tapped with syncing wands.
"Let's make a show!" one cheers and bonds,
And flops like fish, creating fronds.

Under the stars, we shared a spree,
In frosty fun, we all felt free.
Each slip and trip, a joyful decree,
In winter's arms, we danced with glee!

Milton Keynes UK
Ingram Content Group UK Ltd.
UKHW022342171124
451242UK00007B/112